A Flower Burst Open

poems by

Autumn Newman

Finishing Line Press
Georgetown, Kentucky

On average, nearly 20 people per minute are physically abused by an intimate partner in the United States.

A Flower Burst Open

for Pam and Destiny
&
for all who made it out and for all who didn't

ACKNOWLEDGMENTS

Many thanks to the editors of the publications in which the following
poems, sometimes in different versions, first appeared:

Blue Bird Anthology. "He Loves Me; He Loves Me Not"
Cider Press Review. "Reclamation" and "Leaving"
Leo Literary Journal. "Black Birds Flying"
The Orchards Poetry Review. "Push."
Pratik: A Magazine of Contemporary Writing. "Lure," "Shedding Skin,"
"Trying to Call 9-1-1"
Rise Up Review. "Safety Planning Pamphlet"
River Heron Review. "Shame"

This book would not have been possible without the love and support of my
family and the wisdom and skill of my trauma therapist.

These poems would not have been possible without my teachers, especially
the ones who taught me meter and form. The Poetry Witch Community and
the Meter Magic Spiral have been a safe learning and generative space, where
my knowledge of and skill in meter has grown exponentially. The women
there inspire and encourage me to be a better poet.

Publisher: Leah Huete de Maines
Editor: Christen Kincaid
Cover Art: Autumn Newman
Author Photo: Nicky Sabet, Your Moment, My Lens Photography
Cover Design: Elizabeth Maines McCleavy

Order online: www.finishinglinepress.com
also available on amazon.com

Author inquiries and mail orders:
Finishing Line Press
PO Box 1626
Georgetown, Kentucky 40324
USA

Contents

I

Kore Falling

I was lost in their whites when the world was split open.
The narcissus were burning and, falling, I was awoken.
I landed, no longer a maiden. I stood and unfurled—
Persephone, bride of the devil and Queen of the Underworld.

Trapped

The world digests us into women—bleeding, rounded.
Childhood snaps shut and we are pinned insects, jeweled flashes.
Or, falling, we star—our limbs akimbo, reaching wildly.

You caught me and I liked the eagerness behind
your eyes, the readiness to release. I did not know
it was a snare. I did not know I was the rabbit.

More

Cupping my brass heart you drank deep and slow.
Rivulets ran down the sides of your mouth.
Young, I mistook this for passionate love.
Taking my bare hands I tore my chest open—
breaking my sternum, releasing my ribs.
Bleeding and smiling, I offered you more.

Black Birds

I was defenseless against your insidious love—
fiberglass patiently waiting inside of my lungs.

Stuck in my throat, speech fluttered tightly until
I could not hold it inside anymore. Dozens of

black birds flew out of my mouth and into the sky.
But you struck me so hard, that I put them all back.

II

Persephone Eating

Seeds are strange—
burst like breath,
crunch like teeth.

Stained with blood,
lips and tongue
ache with my
swift mistake.

Trickster-God,
coward. He
cannot love.
These slow fires
only take.

Stars

Quick with his fist he silences me.
Thick copper blood is filling my mouth.

I stumble out of the car and into the alley.
The night sky falls

out of my mouth—
bits of teeth, little stars, on the blacktop.

Get in. I'll drive.

He parks at a gas station and walks inside.

I'm stripped, a nerve exposed.
I burn and pulse.

Put this on your lip.

He hands me a styrofoam cup filled with ice.

The violence settles back into itself,
folding, a perfect origami box.

You made me do this.

He pauses for a moment, then starts the car.

The syllables circle.
Shame ripples though me.

Stop crying.

He turns on the radio and drives us home.

My head on the pillow, I thin to mist.
He grabs my hip. I open,
and stars fall out of my mouth.

Push

He pushes into me—

    feral, hard—trying to claim me.

I leave my shell—an ocean

    outcast, drifting blue. The vast

contains me as I cannot

    contain myself. Another home

awaits—in deeper waters—

    where echoes of ancient songs, still thrummed

by giants, will drown me in sleep.

Hands

it was summer

we were standing

cottonwoods were

on the sidewalk

shedding white like

arguing in the

snow

cotton

in a blue sky

when his hands

floating down and down

found my neck

with pure purpose

I could not breathe

swirling

all that cotton

root and grow

Trying to Call 9-1-1

I run into the bathroom, clutching the phone.
My hands are shaking. Against my breasts: the phone.

Couldn't shut the door in time, I should've known.
His hand outstretched, *give me the phone.*

I lie, *I'm just calling home.*
His eyes are glass. *Give me the phone.*

My eyes assault the room. The tub is harder than bone.
Louder now, *the phone!*

He reaches behind and closes the door. We're alone.
I could die in this bathroom. I hand him the phone.

He Loves Me; He Loves Me Not

I am the tulip he peels

Back

petals ripping to reveal

And

snap stigma nectar tipping

Forth

Lure

All my life (it seems) I've been here. On a hook.
Flung here, on the ground, still tonguing the lure in my cheek.
Weight and movement, water flowing through gills, I shook
fin and was gone. Lost. Scales scraped off and lost. I leak
memory of sunlight, jeweled flashes, something
too good not to taste. Bite. Then, the sting and pull.
Body leaving water, flapping wildly. The loud sing
of your fast line reeling, reeling. Too soon I'm dull,
stunned with a hard smack. Now my flat, revenant eyes
swivel, looking for an important answer…but
I've already forgotten the question. Mud brained. Lies.
Lies, you tell me lies. It doesn't matter. Cut
me again. Go deeper. I won't move. Your lure,
the one you threaded so skillfully, is sure.

Home

Smoke hovers, like cobwebs, in the corners of his
childhood home, a yellow brick ranch house.
Immersed in the paper, his mother ignores her
as she stands and moves the chairs to make room
for him at the cluttered kitchen table.
He waits, sits, lights a cigarette, and moves her chair close

to him. He smiles innocently at both of them. Her eyes close.
Gripping the table's edge, with a little sigh, she stands. His
fingers find the fat at the back of her arm. He looks up from the table,
smiles and pinches hard. She squints at the morning sun filling the
  house.
Fuck you she mouths and walks, a little too quickly, into the
  bathroom
where she leans against the counter, back to mirror, and rubs her

arm. She lights a cigarette, shakes the match out, and turns her
head to stare at the closed door, listening to their close
muffled voices arguing in the dining room.
His mother tosses the paper, her voice rising. His
voice stays low. His mother slams the front door. The house
is silent. He slowly pushes his chair back and stands up from the
  table.

Dragged out by the wrist, then backhanded, she lands on the table.
He pulls her back up, and his left fist breaks her
jaw and two of his fingers. The house
spins around her before she blacks out. Noises that are close
sound distant. She sees his boots, feels the spongy seats of his
Chrysler, hears the doors slam. She dreams of her childhood
  bedroom,

yellow and pink. She wakes once in the white emergency room.
When she wakes again, she's in a room with flowers on a table.
The narcotics have worn off. She feels metal in her jaw and sees his
jacket neatly folded over a chair. She follows a tangle of cords to her
call button and pushes it. The nurse swishes in and leans so close

she can smell diet coke on her breath. She mumbles: *When can I go
      home?*

As the car turns the final corner, the yellow house
stands before her. She shuffles straight to her bedroom
while he unpacks the car and then closes
the blinds against the sun. He sits down at the table,
taps out a cigarette and fiddles with his bandaged fingers. Her
bed is worn and familiar. She falls asleep to his

careful movements around the house—his close steps
from room to room, his sitting down and getting up
from the table, his stopping outside her bedroom door to listen.

SAFETY PLANNING PAMPHLET

Important Tips

> *You are not to blame*
> *You are not alone*
> *Help is available*

Document the Abuse

> *Keep a journal (hidden)*
>> Under your eyelids, do not hide it between your legs. He will find it there.
> *Get medical attention and have them document the abuse*
>> Keep the plaster casts, slings, crutches, and stitches in your closet.
> *Make copies of bills for damage to property*
>> This includes your medical bills and death certificate.

Prepare a Safe Room in Your Home

> *Choose a room with a window*
>> Women have been known to fly in desperate circumstances.
> *Have a telephone in that room*
>> Tape God's number to the receiver.
> *Remove weapons*
>> This refers to physical weapons—do not attempt to remove your heart.

III

Persephone Wintering

Not long now, not long—she counts the days
with pomegranate seeds. Not wanting
to part from their tight shell, they burst.
Her hands are stained with their sticky blood,
but she cannot see in the dark. No matter,
soon she will rise and flowers will pop
open behind her as she walks
barefoot on new grass. Freed from winter's
cold hands, the air will bloom and clear
her fetid lungs. The sun will burn
away the fist in her chest and the throbbing
pitch inside of her red valley.
Soon she will find her mother sitting
against an apple tree in a blooming
orchard that smells of honey and leaves.
But for now, she counts seeds in the dark.

Leaving

I was unfolding. I needed nothing.
I left you there on the roadside with nothing.

I was expansive, no longer drowning.
I left you there on the roadside with nothing.

Under the water's surface then breaking.
I left you there on the roadside with nothing.

Filling my lungs until I was shaking.
I left you there on the roadside with nothing.

PTSD: Nightmares

Fear pulls me awake—
a child in shadow waiting
for the dawn to pink.

PTSD: This Body Is Not My Own

Your echo is
unstoppable.

Alone in bed,
I feel your breath.

It swarms and claims
my naked neck.

You crouch in corners,
grinning up at me.

The long day spent
walking around

your feral face,
your long fingers.

Grabbing a wrist,
a chin, a knee,

I twist the bone,
saying out loud:

it's mine, it's mine
it's mine, it's mine…

PTSD: Sex

The me in me fetals,
curling around the already broken,
hushing the edges
as bodies quiver into motion.

Admission

I know, now that it's through,
it doesn't make sense unless…
I loved you before I hated you?

My feelings for you are few—
yes, no. Why retrogress?
I know, now, that it's through.

The intensity springs back, feels new.
I'm afraid of what I possess.
I loved you before I hated you.

Your power lay in what you knew.
Still, I fought hard to suppress
it even before it was through.

I buried what was painfully true—
my full-moon heart, my faithfulness.
I loved you before I hated you.

It was a gun you drew.
My heart caught bullets with finesse.
I know, now that it's through,
I loved you before I hated you.

Shame

Fetal-like, you coiled deep inside of me. You
whisper. I say yes to it all. You tug at
my umbilical, and my body feeds you—
tiny beloved.

Little one, it's decades I've let you live in
catacombs of viscera. I can see my
ribs. My collar bones pull skin tight. You drain me,
bruised and ferocious.

Fading in and out of an anesthetic
dream—the past is pulsing fluorescent light—I
wake to find you here in my hand, no scalpel
needed to loose you.

You are clean and smooth as a stone. You beg a
mother's caress. Something small stalls my fingers.
You were never mine. All I ever needed
to do was let go.

Reclamation

I'm standing knee deep in this deafening river.
Down in the canyon, my voice echoes back to me.
Flooded with pleasure and pain, I shiver.

Ripples are flashing sun and silver,
cutting through mountains down to the sea.
I'm standing knee deep in this deafening river.

Sun-warmed and earthy, sagebrush and juniper
are spinning my senses, branching to memory.
Flooded with pleasure and pain, I shiver.

Striking greens, the Aspen leaves quiver.
Birches bleed—black gashes on every tree.
I'm standing knee deep in this deafening river.

Slick stone, unsteady, I shouldn't linger.
Cool and persistent, the wind nudges me.
Flooded with pleasure and pain, I shiver.

I throw fistfuls of ashes down into the water.
Watching as you disappear is ecstasy.
Standing knee deep in this deafening river,
flooded with pleasure and pain, I shiver.

IV

Persephone Rising

I was once a Goddess who waited for her
season—slowly netting the deep Cocytus.
Now I rise, resplendent in blood-red garnets,
showering hellfire.

Shedding Skin

This is a thunderclap splitting the silence.
This is the lightning bolt thrown.

This is a pain like you could not give to me.
This is the hollow in stone.

This is too seismic, unsteady and sudden.
This is the cracking of bone.

This is a breath that is drenched in the sacred.
This is the rain alone.

This is my body, a flower burst open.
This is the color I've grown.

Unloosed

I am a woman reclaiming her power—
nights on the wing with Goshawks in moonlight,
passing through woodlands bound by the starflower,
weaving through tree trunks, abandoned to flight.

I am a woman reclaiming her power—
straddling the ocean I pull down the darkness.
Swelling to high tide I'm birthing the hour,
sunrise emerges humming to sharpness.

I am a woman reclaiming her power—
running with horses wild on the plain.
Furious, frothing the wind we devour,
powerful hoofbeats unspooling our pain.

Women Who Came Before Me

Beauty is found in the secret places where women breathe fire.

Some of you did not survive, so I hold you in breath between

      water and wave.

Those who survived taught us to live in the stone between

      spark and ignite.

Fury is culled in our secret places; all women breathe fire.

Most of you passed without record, so I listen to marrow; you

      hum in my bones.

All of you spin with the darkness, your heat condensing like

      prayers at birth.

Planets are formed in the secret places where women breathe fire.

Black Birds Flying

We rise, and the blue sky is filled with our song
and the beating of wings in the wind.

We throw shadows, holding the sun on our backs.
We catch wind and release all our weight.

We weave up and down and across. So close
we are one bird trilling the sky.

Notes

National Domestic Violence Hotline
1-800-799-7233

"Safety Planning Pamphlet" print in bold and italics are taken from a pamphlet at a women's shelter in California.

Statistics are from the National Coalition Against Domestic Violence website.

Autumn Newman writes poetry and book reviews. She received her BA in English from California State University, Sacramento and her MFA in poetry from Stonecoast, the creative writing program at the University of Southern Maine. She was an English and creative writing professor at various California community colleges before retiring due to disability. She was Annie Finch's Scansion Assistant for Finch's book *How To Scan a Poem: A Poetry Witch Guide*, and she has mentored women learning meter in Finch's online community, The Meter Magic Spiral. Her work has appeared, or is forthcoming, in *Colorado Review, CALYX Press, Pleiades,* and *The Rising Phoenix Review* among others. This book is the culmination of over a decade of work, trying to recount her experience with domestic violence in a way that is not re-traumatizing for other survivors but that communicates the severity and urgency of this shockingly common form of violence against women.